RUG HOOKING WITH WOOL STRIPS

20 contemporary projects for the modern rug hooker

Katie Kriner

4880 Lower Valley Road • Atglen, PA 19310

Other Schiffer Books on Related Subjects:

Potholder Loom Designs: 140 Colorful Patterns, Harrisville Designs and Rachel Snack, ISBN 978-0-7643-5850-0

Punch Needle Rug Hooking: Techniques and Designs, Amy Oxford, ISBN 978-0-7643-1689-0

Welcome to Weaving: The Modern Guide, Lindsey Campbell, ISBN 978-0-7643-5631-5

© 2021 Design and layout BlueRed Press
© 2021 Text and step images Katie Kriner
Photography by Kate Kriner pp. 37, 107
Photography by Megan Detwiler pp. 37, 65, 107, 115, 127
Cover photograph by Megan Detwiler
Photography by Bob Smith pp. 45, 49, 55, 61, 71, 75, 79, 83, 89, 93, 97, 101, 119, 123
Library of Congress Control Number: 2020952548

All rights reserved. No part of this work may be reproduced or used in any form or by any means—graphic, electronic, or mechanical, including photocopying or information storage and retrieval systems—without written permission from the publisher.

The scanning, uploading, and distribution of this book or any part thereof via the internet or any other means without the permission of the publisher is illegal and punishable by law.

Please purchase only authorized editions and do not participate in or encourage the electronic piracy of copyrighted materials.

"Schiffer," "Schiffer Publishing, Ltd.," and the pen and inkwell logo are registered trademarks of Schiffer Publishing, Ltd.
Produced by BlueRed Press Ltd. 2021
Designed by Insight Design Concepts Ltd.
Type set in Montserrat

ISBN: 978-0-7643-6209-5
Printed in India

Published by Schiffer Publishing, Ltd.
4880 Lower Valley Road
Atglen, PA 19310
Phone: (610) 593-1777; Fax: (610) 593-2002
Email: *Info@schifferbooks.com*
Web: *www.schifferbooks.com*

For our complete selection of fine books on this and related subjects, please visit our website at www.schifferbooks.com. You may also write for a free catalog.

Schiffer Publishing's titles are available at special discounts for bulk purchases for sales promotions or premiums. Special editions, including personalized covers, corporate imprints, and excerpts, can be created in large quantities for special needs. For more information, contact the publisher.

We are always looking for people to write books on new and related subjects. If you have an idea for a book, please contact us at *proposals@schifferbooks.com*.

In memory of my grandmother, whose creative talents inspired her daughters and granddaughters.

Contents

Introduction

Rug hooking is characterized by the pulling or prodding of scraps of yarn or strips of fabric through a backing material. The craft has a complicated history, and like most folk art, there are more legends and myths than evidence. So the history of rug hooking is best understood through the past uses of tools, techniques, and materials.

The Vikings are thought to have introduced the technique of wool loops to western Europe. Other origin theories connect rug hooking to the Bronze Age, Coptic Egypt, and Tudor England, among others. There is also a relationship between rug hooking and rag rug making in Europe and with the early American colonists, where the main purpose was to reuse every scrap of material to make floor coverings.

Forms of rug hooking have evolved and overlapped over time. The variety of antique rugs that survive today shows how they were made and what materials were used. Knowledge was passed down orally, meaning techniques and materials became blended, and the terminology changed regionally as well as through time.

Rugs were sewn with a continuous stitch, pulled with a hook, punched with a hollow needle, or prodded with a tool. While an exact timeline of styles is difficult to establish, rugs were sewn with yarn before 1800, with an increase thereafter in using tools for pulling and punching loops. Rug-hooking techniques developed in North America during the nineteenth century, specifically in the New England states and coastal Canada. The introduction of new materials helped this growth. Jute was being produced on an industrial scale, with much of it woven into burlap and used in feed sacks. The affordable burlap was stronger than wool, cotton and linen and the openings were larger and easier to hook scraps of clothing and other materials. Burlap openings were larger and easier to hook, and the jute was stronger than wool, cotton, or linen. Rug hooking strongly related to household experience, using styles and designs symbolic of everyday life. Motifs captured the family home, domestic animals, flora, fauna, and other elements from the local environment. Rugs were also used to create mementos for significant occasions, such as marriages.

Today, the crafts of punch needle and latch hooking are sometimes confused with rug hooking. While they are similar, the tools and techniques are quite different for all three. Punch needle uses a needle of varying size, depending on the material threaded into it. The maker punches from the back, and the needle creates loops of fixed height on the front. Latch hooking uses a hook-like tool and small strips of yarn that are knotted onto backing fabric, and the maker works from the front.

Rug hooking uses a tool with a wooden handle and a metal hook. The hooker pulls up a wool strip to any height from the front of the piece. The tool itself and the pulling motion are the distinctive features of rug hooking. It is important to make the distinction between these crafts to demonstrate that there is a diverse world of hooking options at your disposal.

As the owner of a rug hooking shop, I address these differences between hooking and punching with my customers on a regular basis. My store, called The Bee & The Bear, is located in an old general store built in the 1850s where I hold classes and host "hookers" regularly. I am always eager to share what I have learned from practicing and teaching rug hooking and interacting with my clients. I hope that through this book, my love of rug hooking reaches a greater audience and that you, my reader, will discover its relevance and true enjoyment.

HOW TO USE THIS BOOK

This book contains twenty wool-strip rug-hooking projects that can be made by beginners or those who have previous experience. While this is not an exhaustive text on rug hooking, it does provide the basics of pattern drawing, pulling loops, and finishing rugs. Each project contains a design, a list of materials, the tools needed, and step-by-step instructions that are the same as I would use when teaching a class. The listed wool colors are suggestions based on what was used in the photographed examples.

The versatility of this craft is shown in the many different types of projects that extend beyond floor usage. My color choices were from hand-dyed wool from my shop, but your choices can make a big impact on the finished product and completely change how your rug will look. Wool sizes and amounts are determined by the artist's measurements and preferences. All in all, this book should be used to inspire and encourage you to hook rugs that express your taste. You should use what you have on hand, but feel free to explore new tools and materials. Please remember there are sometimes several ways to complete a project. Make what you love and enjoy the process!

The patterns can be downloaded as actual-size templates from this site: https://www.schifferbooks.com/rughookingtemplates.

Alternatively, enlarge or reduce the pattern to the size you want by copying and printing it out. The percentage shown beneath the pattern will give the size indicated. If you want to make the template larger or smaller, divide the size you want by the size you have, and turn it into a percentage. For example, if the size you want is 6 in. and length of the pattern is 5 in., $^6/_5$ = 1.20; 1.20 x 100 = 120%. This means you must print out your pattern at 120% (or program the photocopy machine to produce a copy that is 120% the size of the original). Remember, however, that if you make the size larger than the suggestion, you will need more materials.

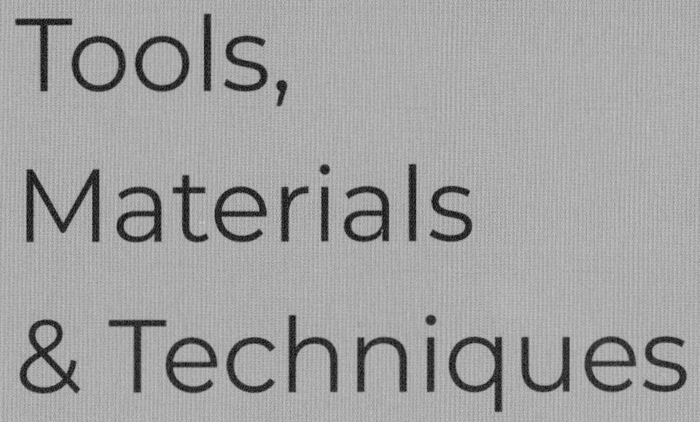

Tools, Materials & Techniques

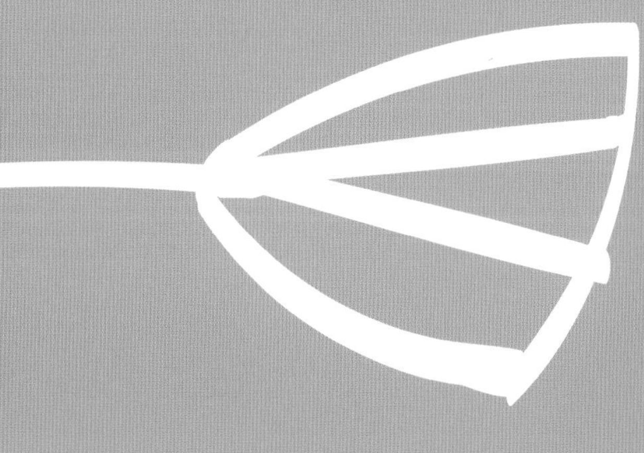

Rug Hooks

Hooks come in many different shapes and size and should feel good and comfortable in your hand, helping you make good loops. Ultimately, the feel and performance should be more important than how the hook looks. Using and sampling a hook is the best way to find out which one is the best fit, but I would also encourage you to ask other rug hookers or store owners. Everyone has an opinion on what works best for them.

How the hook is held differs from artist to artist. Some hold their hook like a pencil, and others grasp it in the palm of their hand. In my shop I have seen all shapes, sizes, and preferences, and it is not uncommon for an artist to have multiple hooks at their disposal. With the variety of hooks available, it is not hard to find a hook that will work with your style of hooking.

Extending from the handle is the metal portion of the hook, referred to as the shank. Some are made from steel and some are made from aluminum. The metal shank can vary in circumference and should correspond to the width of your wool strip. A wide-cut strip is easier to pull up if the shank creates a hole of similar size to the strip. Likewise, a smaller shank works better for smaller cuts of wool. (See the section on cutting wool for more information on cut size; page 12.)

The length of the shank, like the handle, is a matter of preference. The shank can also be straight or bent. This merely aids in the pulling motion and angle of your dominant hooking hand. I prefer a straight hook, but some artists swear by their bent hook. The top of the shank can be like a "J" hook or more like a crochet hook with a little curve to it.

The handle of the rug hook can be made from a variety of materials, including wood, acrylic, or repurposed old tool handles or bone silverware. I prefer wood handles. The more popular varieties of wood-handled hooks are the Hartman hook, made of yew wood, and the Miller hook, made from South American cocobolo wood. Your grip, the size of your hands, and your hooking motion, among other factors, will influence the shape and size of the handle you prefer.

Rule of Thumb: The more scissors, the better. However, you can certainly get by with just the knife-edge appliqué scissors and the dressmaking shears.

Scissors

Scissors are an important part of hooking because they are used in every stage of the hooking process: cutting backing fabric, loops, tails, excess backing fabric, yarn for whipping, etc. Because scissors are used so often, it is important to have good, sharp blades and a comfortable handle. I love my collection of scissors, and below I have listed a few scissors that I use throughout the book.

A. **Gingher Knife-Edge Appliqué**—These are my favorite pair for hooking. They are also known as "duckbill" scissors. The sharp blade is perfect for getting into a loop and making the cut. The curved handle and the flat portion of the blade allow you to place the scissors on the top of your hooking and make a flush, sharp cut.

B. **Dressmaking**—A good pair of dressmaking scissors will come in handy for most of the projects in this book. They are a heavier-duty scissors with longer blades that aid in cutting the bulky backing fabric, yarn, cording, and any other cotton fabrics used for the projects in this book.

C. **Thread scissors**—The first two scissors are necessities for this book, but thread scissors are a nice extra to have when snipping the threads from stitching your binding or sewing your pieces together.

D. **Gingher 5 in. Knife-Edge Scissors**—This is a nice medium-sized scissor—a good little workhorse.

Wool

Wool is a widely used fabric, so it is necessary to describe some details about the kind of wool used in rug hooking. The projects in this book use wool cloth and yarn that is 100% sourced from sheep. Rug hooking is unique because of the process of rendering wool cloth into strips. This is an essential step in preparation for hooking. Therefore, it is important to understand what qualities to look for in a piece of wool.

The wool fabric sourced should be a medium weight and a good weave that is not transparent. I have found this wool should weigh about 1 pound for 1 yard of 60 in. wide wool. All the projects in this book use wool direct from a fabric supplier, but using thrifted wool is a good option. However, there is a bit of preparation involved, and it can be difficult to find the right weight.

Wool is generally categorized in two ways in this book. Mill-dyed wool, sometimes referred to as "as-is" wool, is dyed during production. The fibers are dyed before it is woven into its final pattern, color, or texture. This type of wool is produced on a large scale and distributed on rolls or in bolts. The second category of wool is hand-dyed. This simply means the mill-dyed wool has been overdyed by hand in small quantities (quarters, halves, and sometimes yards). Because of the extra step, this wool produces some great effects in your rug. Hand-dyed wool provides more color options and effects than wool from the mill, which can look flat. Hand-dyed wool is some of my favorite to work with because I can achieve the personal colors, textures, and tones that suit my tastes and make each piece customizable and unique.

Wool Cloth and Rug Hooking in Early America

Today's wool cloth has different uses than in the past. Historically, especially in the American experience, cutting wool into strips was a secondary use for cloth and clothing found in the home or purchased at a shop.

In the eighteenth century, the British flooded the markets of the American colonies with wool cloth. Manufactured, imported cloth far exceeded homemade cloth and yarn by volume. The full impact of this monopoly is not fully understood beyond the fact that local, homemade production of wool cloth was not commercially viable. Precisely when these economic conditions changed to favor making homemade items from stripped wool cloth is currently unknown. However, both the surplus of cloth and attitudes of colonists to reuse clothing seem to support a supply-side theory that the main wool ingredients that we use today for rug hooking were readily available back then.

Colonists in early America had dozens of types of wool cloth at their disposal. Stores along the Atlantic coast were flush with wool cloth and clothing items. The retail business was poised to meet the demands of retail customers in North America with a huge selection and massive choice. At the time, shop keepers, wholesale merchants, and Crown officials did their best to categorize cloth types for accurate bookkeeping and effective marketing. Names used to describe the abundance of wool products can be confusing to today's reader.

Occasionally the names of wool cloth types came to have multiple meanings. Blanket and rug are good examples of cloth originally made for garments but also associated with finished household items for the hearth, floors, or furniture. The term "rug" grew out of the expanding English wool trade as a particular type of cloth merchandise. Rug was a coarse and thick wool cloth that seems to have been more functional than fashionable in North America and the Caribbean. It was popular among the poor social classes, probably because better cloth and clothing materials were continually coming to the market.

Whether rug and similar wool cloth were preferred for making floor rugs because they were cheap, out of style, or easily stripped needs to be explored. As you engage with rug hooking, remember that rug was a kind of wool cloth. Rug hooking today is linked to an appreciation for antique floor and furniture rugs. A broader historical meaning should include a more definitive position for the place of wool cloth in the rug-hooking story. Rug hooking is more about the material used to hook than the end product. This book demonstrates that hooking with wool cloth can be used for much more than making floor rugs.

Dyeing Wool

This book will not cover in detail the various types of dyes or methods used for dyeing wool. The hand-dyed wool in this book used acid dyes—named because of the acid needed to set the color.

Cutting the Wool

There are several ways to cut wool, one being by hand with a rotary cutter or scissors. Hand cutting is time consuming because you are cutting one strip at a time. Such strips will not be uniform but will add character to your rug. Another cutting method uses a machine called at stripper that cuts several strips at a time. Each different cut of wool requires a different blade or cartridge. There are various different models of cutting machines such as Fraser, Beeline, Rigby, Bliss, and Sizzix. If you really enjoy rug hooking, one of these is an excellent investment. I use a Beeline cutter for my rugs and have slowly been adding different sizes of blades/cartridges to my collection.

There are also options for you if you choose not to cut your own wool. One is a rug hooking kit with the wool already cut into strips. A kit has a pattern drawn onto linen with all of the

Dye packets

Wool cutter

Hoops & Frames

You will need a frame or hoop to anchor your backing fabric while pulling the wool through the holes. When starting out, a durable quilting hoop is recommended. They are not expensive, and the hoop does not have to fit the entire rug. The hoop allows you to move your piece around freely and hook the desired section of your project. The key is to pull the backing fabric taut. However, to prevent any creasing, it's best not to leave your rug in the hoop when you are not hooking.

A rug-hooking frame offers a completely different approach to securing backing fabric. This is a wooden frame covered in gripper strips. The gripper strips are similar to wool carding strips and help hold your material taut. This gives you the flexibility to move your piece around much more easily than if it is in a hoop. There are many sizes and shapes, some rectangular and even octagonal. Some frames are made to sit on your lap, while others are attached to a stand. Like your hook, choose one that feels comfortable. I use a lap stand that I lay on my lap while I sit on the couch with my feet propped up on the coffee table.

Take care not to leave the grippers exposed—they are very sharp!

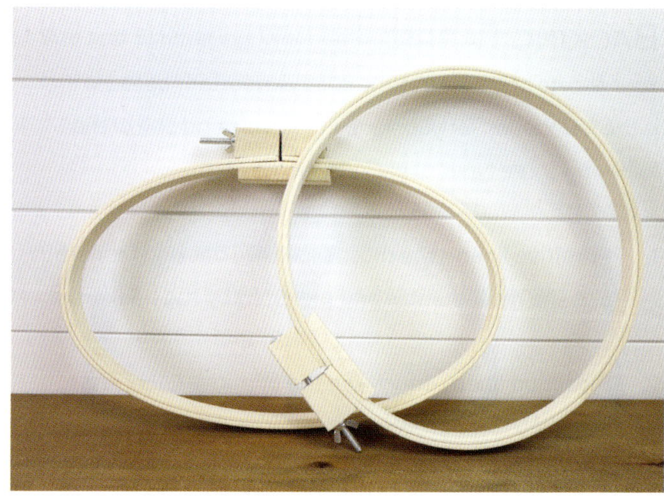

Hoops

Gripper

Other tools and materials used in this book

1. **Steam iron**—A good iron is very important for finishing your rug. I use high steam or a damp towel and press the rug. It makes all of your loops relax together and helps your rug lie flat.

2. **Sewing machine**—The sewing machine is used in several projects in the book. I recommend using heavier-gauge sewing needles such as a $^{90}/_{14}$ or $^{100}/_{16}$.

3. **Serger**—This is a great machine that I use frequently, but it is not something you *must* have for hooking. It simply helps secure the edges of your backing fabric and make seam finishing clean and professional.

Hand-dyed woolen fabric.

4. **Ruler**—Measuring and accuracy with your pattern drawing is very important.
5. **Heavy-duty staple gun**—The stapler is used in several projects in this book. I keep this handy for any project that requires finishing a piece on a frame, or in projects involving upholstery.
6. **Sewing pins**—Good pins are a sewing necessity!
7. **Button or upholstery thread**—Because you are sewing things together that are thick, having good, strong thread is really important.
8. **Sewing needles**—I usually use what I have on hand, but in the course of making the projects in this book, larger needles became my preference. I often choose a yarn-darning needle in sizes 14–18. These still have a sharp tip, but the length of the needle works easily with the thickness of the fabric.
9. **Yarn darner**—For finishing the edge of your rug, you will need a yarn darner that has a blunt tip, but an eye that can hold the thickness of yarn. I use the Chibi jumbo yarn darner needle. This is explained in more detail in the first project of this book.
10. **Sharpie**—This is used for drawing the pattern onto your backing fabric. I use the industrial version for high heat, but a regular black Sharpie will do the trick. Having some other colors is nice, but not necessary if you are making changes to a design already drawn onto the backing fabric.
11. **Lightbox**—For transferring a pattern onto your backing fabric, a lightbox is helpful. Many of the projects in this book used a lightbox for tracing patterns.
12. **Red-dot tracing paper**—This is used to transfer patterns when a lightbox is not available, or wool is being used for the foundation.
13. **Chalk pencil or water / air-soluble fabric pen**—These marking notions are used on cottons when a nonpermanent marking is required.
14. **Sewing clips**—These clips work when pins cannot handle the bulk of the materials.
15. **Rotary cutter**—can be used to cut wool
16. **Binding tape**—1 in. twill tape used on the underside of the rug is one way of finishing. It comes in a variety of colors.
17. **Rug hooks**—come in various sizes and shapes and should meet the artist's preference
18. **Wool fabric**—primary material used to hook a wool rug
19. **Wool-cutting cartridge**—Used in the wool-cutting machines. Each cut requires a different cartridge.
20. **Rug yarn**—100% wool yarn is used for whipping and finishing the edge of the rug.

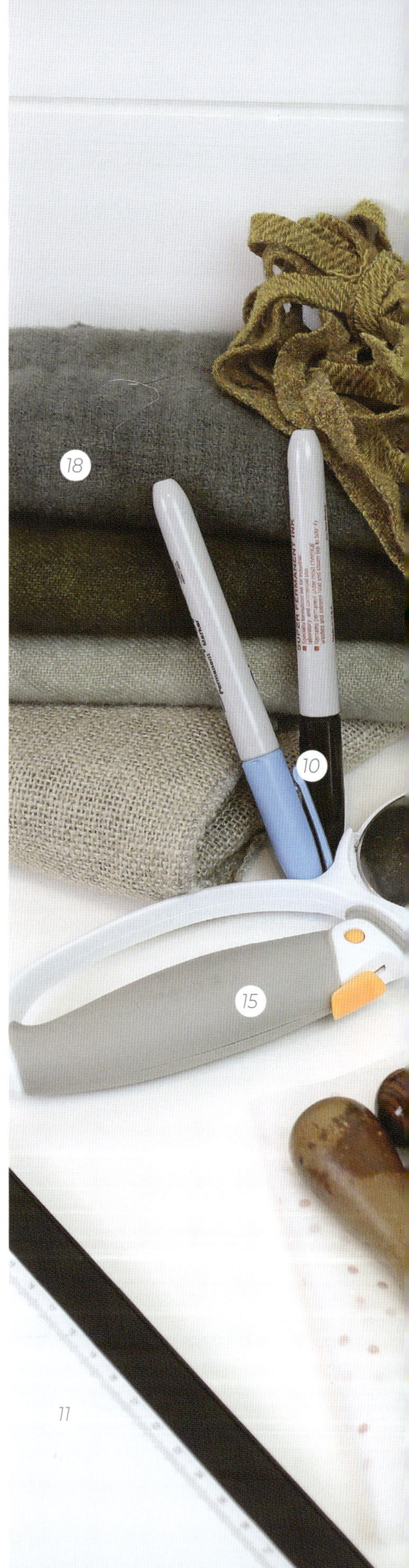

16
5
STANLEY
7
9
4
12
19
6
14
8
20
13

Supply Information

I've made a conscious decision not to publish a list of recommended suppliers, in order to avoid the appearance of favoritism. I'm very willing to make a personal recommendation to you. The Bee & The Bear has grown a strong network of suppliers, store owners, and close friends in the business. I will gladly pass on any specific needs as the situation demands. Discussing through conversation is *always* best.

I encourage you to seek out local rug-hooking stores for individual help, since each rug is a personal work of art. Seeing the color for yourself and feeling the wool makes all the difference—but I realize this is not always possible. A lot depends on where you live.

My shop, The Bee & The Bear, is located in Hereford, Pennsylvania. I have a full selection of rug-hooking supplies and tools—you can find a selection online at *www.thebeethebear.com*. Please get in touch, since I am always willing to correspond via email or talk by phone if you should have questions or need help figuring something out.

The frame used in the Starter Project (back cover bottom right) is a unique item. Similar sifter frames can be ordered from Teresa's Primitive Treasures (*www.teresasprimitivetreasures.com*).

Wools Listed in the Projects

All the hand-dyed colors used in this book are available from my shop. Visit my website for more information.

Unless specifically noted as hand-dyed, the color given is mill-dyed. Like most fabrics, there are limited runs of mill-dyed colors and patterns. While I have tried to use mill-dyed wools that are readily available for all the projects, these will often go out of stock. Your local rug-hooking store should have some good alternative recommendations.

Glossary of Terms

beauty line: A thin line of hooking created by turning a wide wool strip on its side. Used in several projects, but see the Tea Cozy in project 16 on page 108 for directions.

channel: Also referred to as a ditch. These are the rows between the warp and weft of the weave. See "straight of the grain" (*below*) for more information.

cording: Used for whipping the edge of a rug, often polyester cable cord. The size recommended is $^{9}/_{32}$nds.

fat quarter: A quarter of a yard whose dimensions are based on cutting a half yard in half widthwise. Wool that is 60 in. wide will measure 18 by 30 in.

place holder: A strip of wool that is hooked into a piece to hold a space in the design. This is used for letters. Rehooking a line of color helps the color come across crisp and clear.

raw edge: The edge of the linen or backing fabric of choice that is subject to fraying. It is recommended to serge the edge or use some other form of preservation.

selvage: An edge of the linen or backing fabric of choice that has been finished to stop it unraveling

serging: Stopping an edge from fraying by stitching or taping

straight of the grain: The warp and weft threads in material are weaved parallel and perpendicular to the selvage. Keeping the pattern on the straight of the grain is important to keep the rug from twisting.

tails: The end of a strip of wool that is eventually trimmed

worm (a.k.a. noodle): A strip of wool used in rug hooking

Getting Started

Drawing Your Pattern

An important early step of rug hooking, there are three main tools that you need to do draw out your pattern: a Sharpie or black permanent marker, a ruler, and a lightbox or light table.

The most important part is keeping it on the straight of the grain. You should always draw the outer edge of your pattern first, since this will ensure that you stay on the straight of the grain. Linen and monk's cloth have a visible weave, so use this as a guide when drawing the outer border.

First, measure the size of your pattern. Using the starter project in this book as an example (page 28): the tulips are 6 x 10 in. To determine the size of linen you need, add approximately 10 in. to the length and width, so that there is about 5 in. around the outside of your design. So for the tulips, you'll need a piece of linen that is approximately 16 x 20 in. Ideally, also serge the edge of your linen to keep it from fraying. A zigzag stitch or masking tape will also work to preserve the edge.

1. On the linen, mark your outer border. Our example is 16 x 20 in. and the design is 6 x 10 in. Measure 5 in. from the long side of the pattern and mark. Then mark 5 in. on the side.

2. From the 5 in. mark, measure across 6 in. and mark.

3. From the top, measure 5 in. and mark.

4. From the top 5 in. mark, measure 10 in. down and mark.

5. To keep the pattern on the straight of the grain, place your marker tip (or pencil tip) in the channel between two of the threads where you have marked the outer border. Press the marker down and drag the tip in this channel.

6. Do this with all of your marked borders so that they meet and form a rectangle. If you used a pencil, go over this with the black Sharpie.

7. Now you are going to use your lightbox to transfer the rest of the pattern onto the backing fabric. (You could improvise, using a glass-top table or some Plexiglas over two sawhorses with a light underneath.) Place your paper pattern onto the lightbox and tape it to hold it tight.

8. Put your linen over top of the pattern. Line up the outside borders on the paper pattern with what you have drawn on the linen.

9. Draw the inside portion of your pattern. (Use a heavy object or tape to hold the linen in place while you transfer and draw the pattern onto the linen.)

There's another way to transfer patterns: red-dot tracing material that can be purchased in stores or online. To see how this works, have a look at project 5 (page 56)—a pillow that is hooked onto the wool. Note that you will still need to draw your outer border before using the red-dot transfer paper.

This book provides patterns at the start of each project for you to copy. You will need to transfer each to your backing fabric. Alternatively, print them out at actual size from the resources online **(https://www.schifferbooks.com/rughookingtemplates).**

1

SHERWIN-WILLIAMS

2

SHERWIN-WILLIAMS

3

Sharpie
SHERWIN-WILLIAMS
PAINTS

4

SHERWIN-WILLIAMS
PAINTS
VARNISH

5

Sharpie

6

7

8

9

Pulling Loops

To get started, you want your backing fabric pulled as tightly as possible over the gripper strips of your rug frame, or taut in your hoop. The tension will help as you pull the strip through the fabric.

1. While holding the hook in your dominant hand, grasp the strip of wool near the top with your other hand.

2. With your hook on top and your strip of wool underneath, plunge your hook into the backing fabric where you are going to put the wool you have in your hand.

3. Pushing your hook all the way into the material to make a hole big enough for your material to come through can help ease the strain on your hand. You will not hurt the fabric by making the hole larger.

4. Then place the wool from underneath onto the hook and pull it up through the fabric. **(4a)**

   Try to keep it flat and not create twists. Scoop the wool up through the backing fabric. Be sure to catch the whole strip and not just a portion of it. **(4b)**

5. With your hook, bring the end of the strip fully through to the front.

6. This end is called your "tail" and should be sticking up on the front right side of your backing fabric about ½ in. high.

7. Push your hook back into the fabric in the hole adjacent to the first strip.

8. Using the same technique as before, bring up a loop from the strip of wool below. Place the wool onto the hook from below and pull up the loop. Remember to make sure the whole piece of wool is being caught by the hook.

9. To make the next loop, place your hook back into the fabric, skipping a hole. Counting holes is fine to start, but once you get the hang of it, just pull loops to fill in the area without counting. **(9a)**

   If your strips are narrow, they will be closer together. If your strips are wider, more space will be needed between your loops. **(9b)**

10. A general rule is to pull your loops as high as they are wide. So, if you are using a #8 cut, your loops should be ¼ in. high.

1

2

3

4a
6
9a
4b
7
9b
5
8
10

11. As you make loops, you will eventually reach the end of the wool strip. Pull this end of the strip to the front, just as you did at the start of the strip.

12. To start your next wool strip, put your hook into the same hole where the last strip ended. You will have two tails sticking out of the same hole. **(12a)**

    Pull up a tail as you did with your first strip, and start pulling loops in succession. **(12b)**

13. To end before your strip is used up, just pull a loop up a little high and cut it. **(13a)**

    Pull the rest of the strip from below and out of the fabric. **(13b)**

14. Your tails or ends of the strips will be sticking up. **(14a)**

    Simply cut these tails flush with the rest of the loops. The wool will fluff out and blend in with the rest of the loops around it. **(14b)**

15. You can also end or start your color against another loop or tail already pulled up to the front. Generally, you want your starting and ending tail to be in the same hole.

    Starting or ending right next to another row or loop is also acceptable.

16. Typically, I will hook the outline of a feature and then fill it in. In this case, I hooked the outside of the leaf and then filled in the loops. I did the same for the outer border of the rug, then hooked all the way around and finally filled in the inside.

    Tails should not end at the edge of a rug either. Otherwise the tail could possibly get caught or be easily pulled out.

17. No tails or ends should be left on the back of the rug. The tails should be on the top and cut flush with the rest of your loops. This is so the end does not get caught from the back and cause the loops to unravel. When the tails are all at the top, they are protected by the other loops from loosening.

    The back of your rug should be flat anyway, in addition to no tails being left on the back. You do not want to carry a piece of wool over something that has already been hooked. This would create a lump that could also get caught or wear unevenly and break.

11

12a

12b

13a
14b
17
13b
15
14a
16

4. The tail of the yarn should be whipped into the cording and backing fabric as you go. This will hide any loose ends.

5. Continue whipping the edge of the rug. Your yarn loops should be even: don't make them exceedingly tight, just snug. I like to put my needle into every hole as I go along, to keep consistency and to ensure that the yarn evenly and fully covers the backing fabric and cording.

6. Corners take a bit of patience, practice, and caution. You will be whipping in a little bit of excess as you go around. I like to put my yarn through a couple of the holes twice on my way around the corner to ensure full coverage.

7. When you get to the end of the yarn, whip until you do not have enough left to go around. Rethread your needle with another yard-long piece of yarn.

8. To start the new piece of yarn, slide the needle through a section of whipped yarn on the back and start again.

9. As you start a new piece of yarn, hide that tail by whipping the previous tail in with the cording and backing.

10. Continue all the way around the rug. When you get to the point where the two tails are overlapping, snip them so they are just touching, and secure the ends with a little clear tape to keep them from fraying. **(10a)**

    These two ends must be right next to each other: too short and there'll be a gap, then the rug will bend at this spot. Too long and they will overlap, leaving a visible bump. Neither eventuality is good. **(10b)**

11. Once you have your ends nice and close, whip the rug the rest of the way down, covering up all cording and backing fabric so there are no gaps.

4

5

6

7
10a
8
10b
9
11

12. To end your yarn, bring it to the back as if you are making a final loop, then sew it through some of the previous whipped section. **(12a)**

    Clip the yarn as close as possible and massage the end into hiding. **(12b)**

    A well-bound rug has no visible starting or stopping points and no visible tails. **(12c)**

12a

12b

12c

Finishing with Rug Binding

Another great way to finish your rug is to use a process known as rug binding. This produces a clean edge at the end of your hooking and gives a nice hemmed finish on the back.

1. After you have finished hooking your rug, give your piece a good steam press to help it lie flat. Trim the excess backing fabric to 1 in. away from the edge of the hooking. You can use the serger to do this for you.

2. Using your steam iron, press the backing fabric to the back of your piece.

3. Open the flap at the corner and fold the corner inward. Press. Do the same for all four corners.

1

2

3

4. Next you are going to miter the corners by folding the sides in to create a triangle.

4

5. Pin to hold in place. Sewing clips are also helpful here. Pin all four corners down. The small gap will be closed when it is stitched.

5

6. Using strong upholstery or button thread, start stitching the corners and backing fabric.

6

7. I like to start at the corner and then work my way around the rug, using a simple whip stitch to tack everything down into place. **(7a)**

   When you get to the end, finish and knot your thread. **(7b)**

8. Measure out the amount of rug binding you need, and cut. For safety, bind the end with clear tape to stop it fraying.

9. Lay the rug binding flat on the edge of your rug and start by stitching it into place, using a whip stitch. Catch a little bit of the backing fabric and a little bit of the binding.

10. Continue all the way up the side to the corner.

11. Turn your binding to the next side by creating a triangle at the corner. Pin the triangle into place.

7a

9

7b

10

8

11

12. As you work your way around, attaching the binding on the outside, pin the corners and inside as you go. **(12a)**

    When you get to where the two ends of the binding meet, fold the top binding piece over to create a clean edge. The fold should be no more than an inch. **(12b)**

13. Stitch the end of the folded binding down and move onto the inside portion.

14. Stitch the inside and each corner, using the same whipping stitch as you used on the outside.

12b

13

12a

14

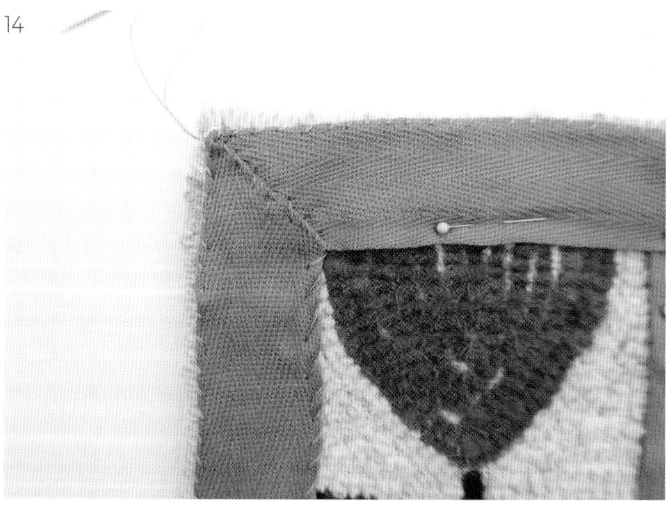

Projects

4. The watering can is hooked with a hand-dyed wool that has shades of grays and greens. Hooking this created the aged look of a well-used watering can. This is an example of where a well-chosen piece of wool does all the hard work of coloring for you.

   Notice that the background was hooked going *around* the watering can, so the hooking direction of the background allows the eye to travel around the watering can and see movement as a prominent characteristic of the rug. The same can be said for the rain boots.

5. Both pieces are finished using the backing fabric to create a hem, so the following instructions will apply to the rain boots and the watering can. A good steam iron is needed for a successful finish. Start by trimming the backing fabric to 2 in. from the edge of the hooked rug.

6. Using a pencil, drag the tip in the channel or simply measure and mark all the way around the rug. Trim at the 2 in. mark. Serge this edge if possible.

7. Measure 1 in. from the corner. **(7a)**

   Draw a diagonal cutting line, then trim to cut off the triangle. I also recommend serging this edge if possible. **(7b)**

8. Fold all the corners into the back and press.

9. Fold the sides over and press.

10. Fold the sides in half so that the raw or serged edge is tucked inside. Give this a good press as well.

11. Line up your corners and pin everything into place.

4

5

6

7a

7b

8

9

10

11

12. Starting at one of the corners, stitch the hem into place, using strong upholstery or button thread and small whip stitches. A long darning needing with a sharp point is my preferred tool for this.

A third tray would have been perfect for project 6 (on page 62), but using barn wood to frame the shovel and trowel was the right touch for that project. Always remember, inspiration can strike at any time, anywhere.

12a

12b

Project 3: Bird in Foliage Pillow

Birds are a very popular theme in hooked rugs, and I wanted to incorporate them into this book since I enjoy watching them out my kitchen window. I also love pillows, since they can add a lot to the décor of a home.

In this piece, the entire front is hooked, which gives the pillow a bit of weight. I have a large dog, and I want my pillows to have some heft so they stay put when she gets up on the couch. I used leftover backing fabric, wool strips, and other unusable scraps of fabric for stuffing. The semicircular shape (sometimes referred to as a tombstone in rug hooking), also makes this pillow unique. In fact, it's the perfect shape for an upholstered armchair.

To achieve a finished size of 12 in. x 16 in. download a template or copy and print this pattern at 457%.

Materials & tools needed:

Linen—about 22 x 26 in.

Wool—(Background Cut #9, Bird & Foliage Cut #8)

- 1/16 yd. mixed greens
- ½ yd. hand-dyed off-white ("Wooly Sheep")
- 1/16 yd. mixed hand-dyed blues
- 8 strips of hand-dyed golden brown ("Honey")
- 3 strips of hand-dyed light brown ("Acorn")
- 10 strips of white
- Strip of dark blue for the wing accent
- Strip of dark brown or black for the eye
- Strip of gold for the beak

Décor fabric for back of pillow, 14 x 18 in.

Hook + scissors

Needle + thread

Serger—optional

Sharpie permanent marker

Stuffing—of choice

1. Start out by drawing your pattern onto the backing fabric using a lightbox. Keep the bottom line straight on the grain by drawing your line in the channel or ditch of the linen. Hook the piece, using the colors of your choosing.

   To keep the bird's eye small, simply pull up two tails and snip. The beak was done by pulling up a tail, a loop, then another tail, and massaging them into the shape of the beak.

2. I added a "beauty line" on the wing to make it stand out a little. You can find instructions on how to make a beauty line in the Tea Cozy project on page 109.

3. Once you have finished hooking and have given your piece a good press with the iron, trim the backing fabric to about 2 in. from the edge of the hooking.

1

2

3

4. Pin the backing fabric to the hooked portion of your rug, right sides together.

5. Using a sewing machine, a heavy-duty needle (14 or 16), and a zipper foot, sew as close as you can to the edge of the hooking, leaving the bottom of the pillow open.

6. Turn the pillow right side out and check your sewing.

7. Because you cannot put the sewing-machine foot right next to the hooked part without catching the wool, there will be a small section of the linen showing. You can carefully hook another row into that section if you wish, or leave it as a narrow border. This will hardly be seen anyway, because of the curvature of the pillow.

8. If you are satisfied, turn the pillow inside out and trim the seams to about ½ in. If you have a serger, this is a great way to secure the seam.

9. After trimming, turn right side out and stuff the pillow. I wanted a firm, heavy pillow, so I used leftover scraps of backing fabric and wool pieces. Pin the bottom of the pillow together and hand-stitch together.

5

6

4

7

8

9

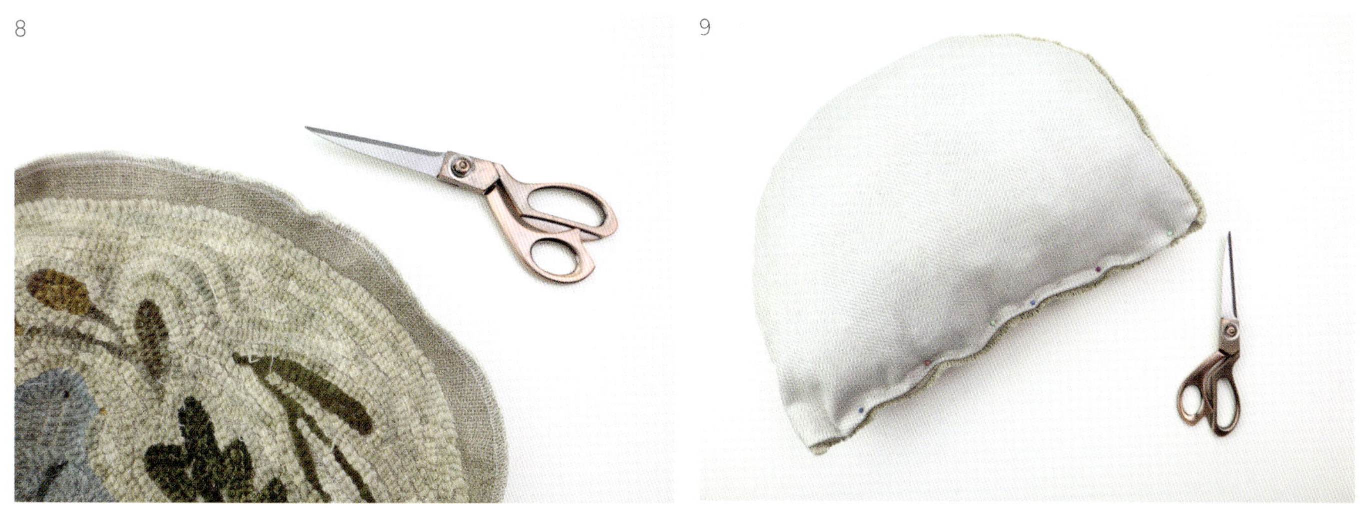

Project 4: Blue Flower Pillow

The concept for this pillow came from the desire to turn a small mat into a pillow. The hooking portion is small and not overwhelming, and the finish is beautiful and useful at the same time. I found that sewing the wool for the pillow on first is the easiest way to approach this project. This way, the wool strips can be hooked right up to the edge of the wool without any backing fabric showing, saving the hassle of fitting the wool fabric around the hooked portion afterward.

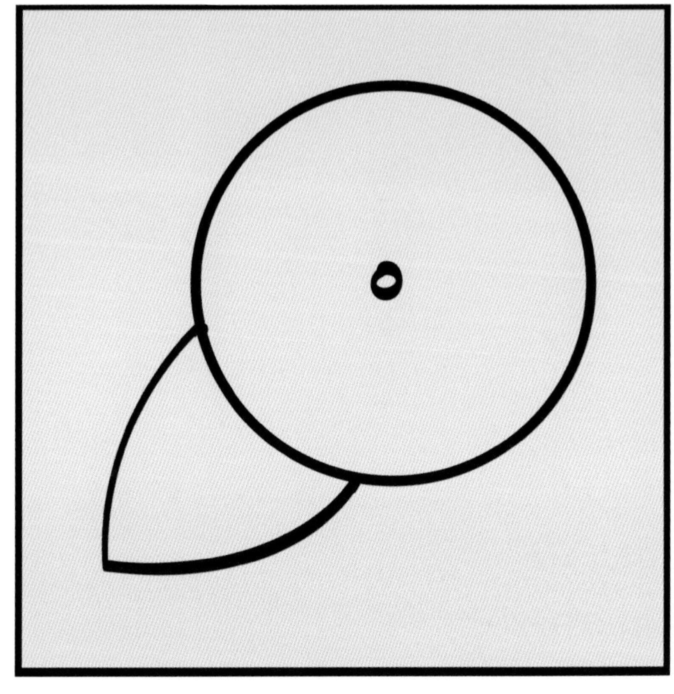

To achieve a finished size of 12 x 12 in., download a template or copy and print this pattern at 343%.

Materials & tools needed:

Linen—18 in. square

Wool—(cut #8)

- ½ yd. brown plaid for pillow backing—the best dimensions are an 18 x 60 in. half
- 1/16 yd. white wool
- 5 strips of hand-dyed dark-green wool ("Dark Olive")
- 1 strip of off-white for center of flower
- 1/32 yd. hand-dyed light blue ("Winter Lake")

12 in. square pillow form

Hook + scissors

Serger (optional)

Sewing machine

Sharpie permanent marker

1. Using your lightbox, draw a 7 in. square along the straight of the grain onto your backing fabric. Then draw the design in the center.

2. From the selvage edge, measure up 10 in., snip, and tear straight across.

3. Next, tear the piece for the front of the pillow. Measure up 14 in., snip, and tear. You will also need the second piece for the back: measure 10 in. up, snip, and tear.

   There are now three pieces in total—two that are 10 in. and another that is 14 in. The width of these three pieces will be your half yard of about 18 in., depending on how much the wool has shrunk in the wash cycle (see page 12 for cutting and washing details).

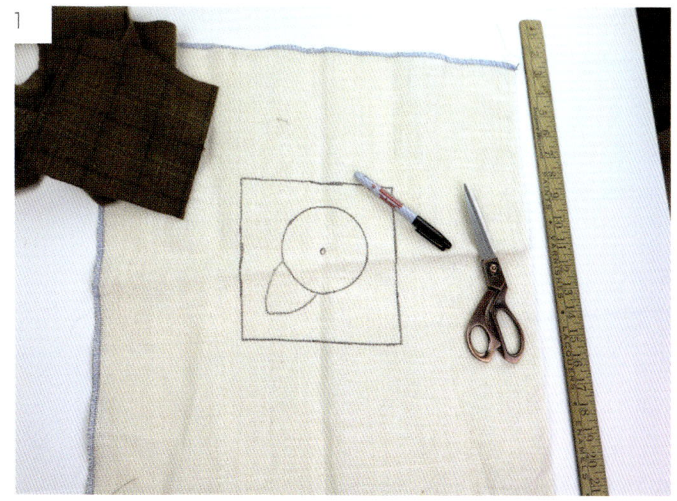
1

2

3

10. Lay the bottom half of wool from step 3 on top of the pillow. Line up the bottom edge with the bottom edge of the pillow. Pin into place to temporarily hold them together. Ideally, your top and bottom should overlap by about 5 in.

11. Flip your piece over and pin into place on the linen side. The hooked section needs to be centered on the pillow. For a 12 in. pillow, measure and mark a border of 2½ in. all the way around the hooked square: this is your sew line. Remove the pins from the other side.

12. Sew all four sides of the pillow.

13. Flip the pillow right side out and check to be sure everything lines up. Turn the pillow inside out, trim any excess seam allowances, and clip the corners.

14. If you have a serger, this is a great place to give your piece a professional finish by serging all the seams.

15. Flip the pillow right side out and insert your pillow form.

11

12

10

13

14
15

Project 5: Wool-Base Flower Pillow

This pillow takes the concept of hooking right into the wool as your base material—the wool is your background. While this is not difficult, I would recommend hooking in linen first, since this is a more advanced technique that requires a good handle on basic loop making.

Wool is not as forgiving a base as linen, so some hooking experience is invaluable. With linen, you can remove a row or loop without worrying about leaving evidence of an error. When hooking into wool, the hole is pretty permanent. So, when you are hooking your stems, you have only one chance to get them right. If you remove the row for the stem and move it somewhere else, you will leave behind some visible holes. I suggest starting with the grassy area to get the hang of this method.

A little preparation at the beginning sets you up for a good envelope pillow construction, with two seams to sew together. A pillow form completes the look.

To achieve a finished size of 16 x 16 in., download a template or copy and print this pattern at 457%.

Materials & tools needed:

Wool for pillow—20 x 40 in.

Wool for hooking (cut #8)

- Grass + stems, 1/8 yd. hand-dyed green ("English Garden")
- Stems, 1/16 yd. hand-dyed dark green ("Deep Forest")
- Light blue, 1/32 yd. hand-dyed ("Winter Lake")
- Dark blue, 1/32 yd. hand-dyed ("Delft Blue")

16 in. pillow form

16 in. square of red-dot tracing fabric

Hook + scissors

Sewing machine

Sewing pins

Sharpie marker

1. Start by laying the red-dot tracing fabric on top of your paper pattern, aligning the bottom of the pattern with a row of red dots. Trace the pattern onto the red-dot fabric, using a black marker pen.

2. Measure up 12 in. from the bottom (short end) of the 20 x 40 in. piece of wool. (I like to keep the selvage edge at the top of this piece so I can use it as the finished edge on the back.) Place the red-dot fabric with your pattern onto the wool, with the bottom edge of the pattern at the 12 in. mark. Be sure to center your design on the wool. By all means, use a few sewing pins to secure it in place if you are worried about slippage.

3. To transfer the pattern, press down with your Sharpie and trace over the entire pattern. Working on a hard surface helps with the transfer, but you may need to go over some of the lines again to firm them up after you remove the red-dot paper.

1

2

3

4. Begin hooking your piece. Push the hook into the wool just as you would do with the linen. Pull your tail. **(4a)**

   Make a loop and so forth. As I suggested earlier, I recommend starting on a larger section such as the grass, to get the hang of hooking on wool since it is not as forgiving as linen. Only then move on to the flowers. **(4b)**

   Generally, you do not want tails hanging out in the open, so try to plan for this when you hook. Do not end the edge of the grass with a tail, since there will be no other loops around it to hold it in. **(4c)**

5. Once you have finished your hooking, you are ready to start constructing the pillow. With the right side facing up, fold the top portion of the wool down and onto the hooked flowers.

6. Next, fold the bottom up, overlapping the top. **(6a)**

   Measure from the top and bottom fold lines to ensure there is 16 in. **(6b)**

   Add some pins along the side and turn it over to check that the front side is also 16 in. Pin this side along the edge and remove the pins from the other side. **(6c)**

7. Measure the width and mark 16 in. across so that the design is centered within the 16 in. **(7a)**

   Mark the seams for easier sewing. **(7b)**

4a

4b

4c

9
12
10
13
11
14

15. Put your hook in next to the first loop from step 14 and pull a second loop the same height as the first.

16. Leave the tails for the bee wing on the back. Trim them to about 1–2 in. long.

17. Once you have finished hooking, press your piece, including the backing fabric, so the piece is nice and crisp. Notice that I have also left the ends of the saucer on the back because I did not want loose ends on the front. Lay your stretcher bar frame on the back.

18. Using thumbtacks or pushpins, tack the linen into place.

19. Once you are satisfied with the positioning, use your staple gun to secure the linen to the stretcher bar.

20. Trim any excess linen from the back. You may cover the back up with a piece of fabric or matte board, using a staple gun. Add a sawtooth hanger to the top.

16

17

15

18

19

20

Project 8: Six Flowers Large Floor Rug

When you think of rug hooking, a floor covering probably immediately comes to mind. This piece is a simple design that can be made larger or smaller by adding or removing flowers, and even shortening or lengthening the stems. I stuck with neutral tans, greens, and blues because I did not want to take away from the simplicity of the design. This is a perfect project for those who want some flexibility in size and color.

To achieve a finished size of 22 x 30 in., download a template or copy and print this pattern at 625%.

Materials & tools needed:

Linen—about 32 x 40 in.

Wool—(background & border cut #9, flowers cut #8.5)

- Flowers: 3/16 yd. hand-dyed light-blue wool ("Melrose")
- Stems + leaves: 1/4 yd. hand-dyed dark green ("Dark Olive")
- Outer border: 1/2 yd. hand-dyed dark brown ("Pebble Brown Dark")
- Background: 1 1/4 yd. hand-dyed light brown ("Pebble Brown")

3 yd. x 9/32 in. cording

Hook + scissors

Rug yarn, hand-dyed dark brown ("Pebble Brown Dark—BBY81")

Serger

1. Using a lightbox, draw your pattern onto the linen. Draw both the outer (22 x 30 in.) and the inner (18 x 26 in.) rectangle first and then add the flowers. I started hooking the flower heads first.

2. The stems came next, followed by the leaves. Hook the outline of the leaf first and then fill the inside in with loops.

3. To keep the rug in its rectangular shape, I hooked a row along the border of the background and then filled in with loops. This outside row is called a "holding line" because it gives the edge a nice and tidy line to hook up to and visually frames the piece.

1

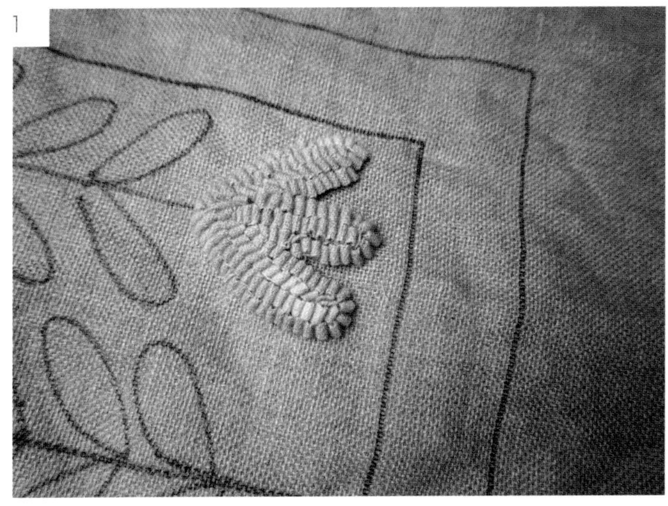

2

3

4. The leaves and in-between gaps take a bit of time to hook because there are lots of curves.

5. For this piece, I had started with a different, darker wool for the background. But I felt my leaves were getting lost. The wools all looked good together, but when they were right next to each other in loop form, it was not a good match; they became too close in tone.

6. I simply pulled out the strips in what is sometimes referred to as "reverse hooking."

7. There will be larger holes in the linen after you take out the wool, but you can use your fingernails to push the fibers back into place. These disappeared when a better background was hooked.

8. For the border, I chose to hook a thin line of the green from the flower stems right next to the background. I hooked the border next, ensuring that each row was as straight as possible.

9. This rug was finished with cording and yarn in a color that matched the border.

5

6

4

7

8

9

3. Leave both ends open to create a long tube.

4. Pack the tube with stuffing of your choice. To make this piece heavy, use cut-up pieces of scraps such as backing fabric, wool strips, and even lint from the dryer. Because this is a long piece, you will need to stuff from both ends, so use something like a dowel rod to pack it in really well.

5. Next, fold in the linen at either end of the tube and pinch it together to close the seam. **(5a)**

   Close the ends up, using a ladder or whip stitch. **(5b)**

4

5a

3

5b

Project 11: Zippered Clutch Bag

In my pursuit of making functional items, I wanted to make a clutch with a zipper. This is not something you typically see hooked. The obstacle was finding a way to attach a zipper to a hooked-rug project. After several models and attempts, I found that the best way to combine the bulk of a rug and a zipper is to tackle the zipper first.

Zippers can be intimidating, but the zipper placement in this piece is fairly straightforward, with straight sewing lines for attachment. The materials listed are approximates and can be customized to your bag size of choice. Zippers come in many different sizes, and I recommend purchasing a strong, well-constructed zipper, made with metal or very heavy plastic teeth, that will open and close with ease.

Materials & tools needed:

- Linen—about 10 x 15 in.
- Cotton—2 x 10 x 15 in. for the lining
- · 1/8 yd. of wool strips in your chosen colors
- Fabric—10 x 15 in. for the back of the bag
- Hook + scissors
- Sewing machine
- Sewing pins
- Sharpie
- Strong zipper (10 in. for the triangle clutch)
- Thread of suitable color

To achieve a finished size of 4 x 10 in., download a template or copy and print this pattern at 250%. For 5 x 9 in., print at 225%.

1. Start by attaching the zipper. Begin by laying the zipper facedown on the top edge (15 in. side) of your linen. Line up the edge of the zipper to the edge of the linen.

2. Next, lay a piece of the cotton facedown on the zipper. Line up the 15 in. edge with the 15 in. edge of the linen. The zipper should be sandwiched between these two layers. Pin everything together.

3. Sew along the edge of the zipper, using a zipper foot on the sewing machine. Stitch about ¼ in. away from the zipper teeth.

1

2

3

4. Press the cotton material back, then stay-stitch into place, catching the zipper tape and hem of the linen.

5. Next, using the other side of the zipper, place the zipper facedown on the fabric for the back of the bag. Lay the cotton fabric facedown on the wrong side of the zipper.

6. Pin and sew about ¼ in. away from the zipper teeth. Stay-stitch the lining to the zipper tape and seam of the back fabric to prevent the lining from getting caught in the zipper. Stay-stitch the lining to zipper tape and the fabric for the back of the bag. This will help prevent the lining from getting caught in the zipper.

7. Flip the bag so that you are looking at the front linen, with the zipper facing up. Draw lines on the linen straight down from the end of both the top and bottom zipper stops. The lines should be the same length and will depend on how deep you want the bag to be (these clutches are both 4 in. deep). Connect the ends of the two lines by drawing the bottom of the bag.

8. Draw the pattern onto your bag.

9. Place the linen onto your frame or in your hoop to hook.

10. Hook right up against the top edge of the bag and straight down from the zipper stops.

4

5

6

7

10

8

11

9

11. Once you have finished hooking, you can stitch up the bag. Put all right sides together. Match your hooked front to the fabric for the back of the bag, and match the cottons together. Pin, starting at the zipper, and make sure to match the outer fabrics at the zipper and fold the zipper teeth toward the lining. Pin down the side, working your way out to the end of the hooked purse, pinning along the bottom of the hooked portion. (Put the pins on the opposite side of the hooked portion. This will allow you to put the foot right up against the hooking without catching the hooked loops.)

12. Pin the sides of the cotton, leaving the bottom edge open. Be sure to open the zipper about three-quarters of the way before starting to sew the bag; this way you will be able to flip it right side out once you have finished sewing.

13. Using the sewing machine and the zipper foot, stitch the bag—starting from one side of the cotton and going around to the other side of the cotton.

14. Flip the purse right side out to check that everything has been sewn properly. Flip it inside out and trim all of your seams. If you can serge the edges, do so.

15. To finish the lining, pull it out from the bag. Measure how deep the purse is, then trim the lining about an extra ½ in. longer.

16. Tuck the raw edge about ¼ in. inside the bag. Press and top-stitch to close the edge.

12

13

14

15

16

Project 12: Fern Purse with Cutout Handle

The inspiration for this purse came from seeing a cutout purse made from fabric alone. I immediately wanted to make one that was hooked, but I had to figure out if it would work. It was a process of trial and error, but in the end, I achieved the look I wanted.

Cutting out the circle from within a hooked piece presents challenges because the linen will fray if not secured properly. Therefore this does require a bit of hand sewing. The handwork is really what pulls the bag together to make it look clean and crisp. I made the purse large enough to fit an iPad or paperback book, but it could also work for a night out. Finished size is 10 x 11 in.

Materials & tools needed:

Linen—20 x 36 in.

Wool—(background cut #9, fern cut #8)

- ½ yd. hand-dyed off-white ("Wooly Sheep")
- 1 yd. hand-dyed medium brown ("Acorn")

Chibi yarn darner needle

Darning needle

Hook + scissors

Strong button thread or upholstery thread

Whipping yarn

To achieve a finished size of 10 x 11 in., download a template or copy and print this pattern at 312%.

1. Draw two rectangles on the straight of the grain, 10 in. tall x 11 in. wide, onto your backing fabric—leave about 4 in. between the two. **(1a)**

   Draw the cutout portion at the top: first marking 1 in. from the top, 3 in. from the sides, and then 1.5 in. from the 1 in. line. **(1b)**

   Connect all of these marks to form a rectangle. Draw the fern onto your pattern, using a lightbox. **(1c)**

2. To make the curved handle, draw a semicircle at either end of the rectangle.

3. You must zigzag the handle. Use a tight zigzag and go right over the line you drew in steps 1–3. Do this on both of the 10 x 11 in. rectangles, so you have two matching sides.

1c

1a

2

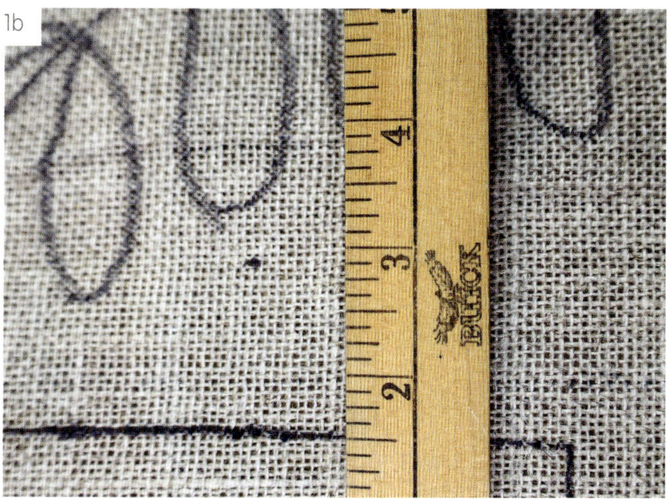
1b

3

4. Hook both rectangles, leaving the oval cutout unhooked. Hook right up to the zigzag line on the oval. Trim your piece about 1 in. from the edge of the hooking on the sides, and 2 in. at the top. Serge the edge. Fold the top over twice to create a hem, and press into place. Then, whip-stitch the hem down. It will meet the edge of the oval cutout space.

5. Place both layers' wrong sides together, carefully lining up the top and bottom corners.

6. Using a ladder stitch (also known as slip stitch, blind stitch, or invisible stitch), sew up the sides and bottom.

7. A nice, close ladder stitch will produce a hidden seam.

8. For the cutout handle, cut the linen out from inside the oval. Trim up to the zigzag line. Using the rug yarn, encase the zigzag edge in yarn by whipping it around the stitching. **(8a)**

   This will give the edge a clean and secure finish. **(8b)**

5

6

4

7

8a

8b

Project 13: Easter Eggs

These eggs allow for lots of creative flexibility. This project is one of the quickest hooks in the book. I ended up making more than originally planned because I could not help myself! They go pretty fast, and the construction is simple. You can use up leftover wool and also smaller pieces of linen to combine colors and make any pattern you like. Make them bigger or smaller—it is up to you! Put them in a bowl or basket for the perfect Easter centerpiece.

To achieve a finished egg size of 4.5 x 6 in., download a template or copy and print this pattern at 658%.

Materials & tools needed:

Linen—24 in. square will make about four eggs

Wool strips—(cut #8, 8.5)

- Mix of pastel colors. Each egg uses about 1/16 yd.
- Wool for backing each egg. Each needs a piece about 5 x 6.5 in. for a 6 in. tall egg

Hook + scissors

Needle + thread

Paper for tracing pattern

Sharpie

Stuffing of choice

1. Draw the egg outline onto the backing fabric and the design. Hook the design.
2. Cut the eggs out, leaving a 2 in. border all the way around.

3. Fold the backing fabric toward the back of the egg and press in place.

4. Trace the shape of your egg onto a piece of paper.

5. Cut the paper egg out and lay it on top of the egg to make sure it fits. (Sometimes when hooking, the piece can end up being a little smaller or larger than the originally drawn shape, so the back wool should be cut to fit each individual egg you hooked.)

3

1

4

2

5

6. Lay the paper pattern onto the wool and pin in place. **(6a)**

   Cut around the paper egg pattern. **(6b)**

7. Lay the fabric on the back of the egg and pin into place.

8. With a needle and thread, hand-stitch the wool egg and hooked egg together, leaving a 2 in. opening.

9. Stuff the egg. Use poly-fill stuffing or wool scraps.

10. Sew the 2 in. opening shut the rest of the way.

7

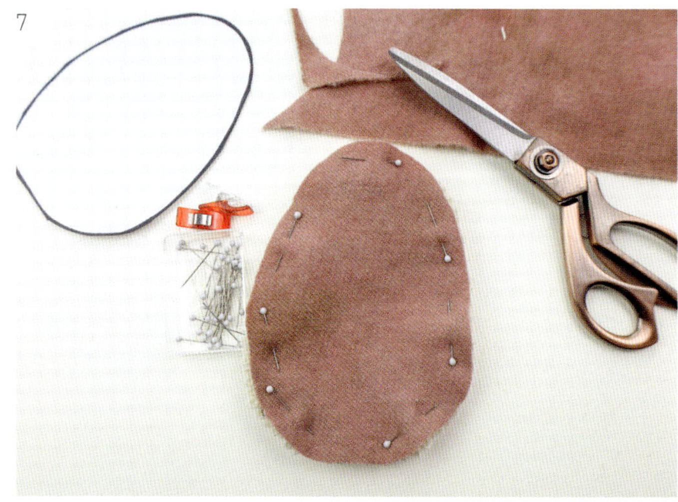

6a

8a

6b

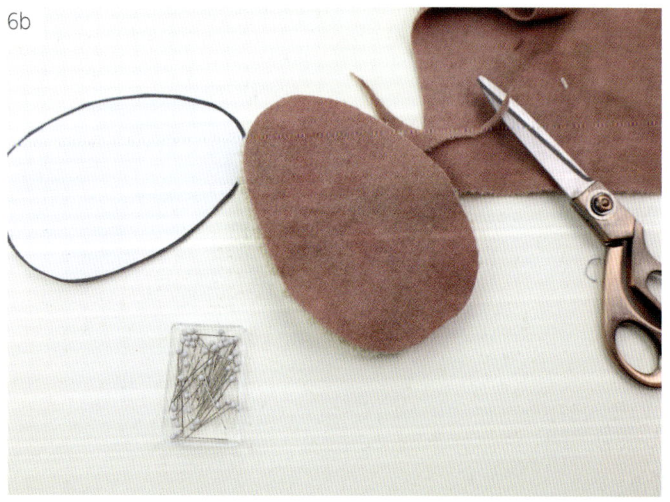

8b

9

10

Project 14: Candy Corn Bowl Filler

Candy corn is a classic Halloween treat and a perfect size for a bowl or display. This candy corn differs from the Easter eggs because both sides of the candy corn are hooked. Hand sewing is required to put these together, but the final product is well worth the effort. The three-dimensional look is very cool. Mix and match colors if you like, or stick to the traditional look.

Materials & tools needed:

Linen—24 in. square makes about three small candies

Wool—¼ yd. of wool (cut #8)

- Mix of white, yellow, and orange colors

Hook + scissors

Needle + strong button or upholstery thread

Serger (optional)

Sewing clips

Sewing machine

Sharpie

Stuffing of choice

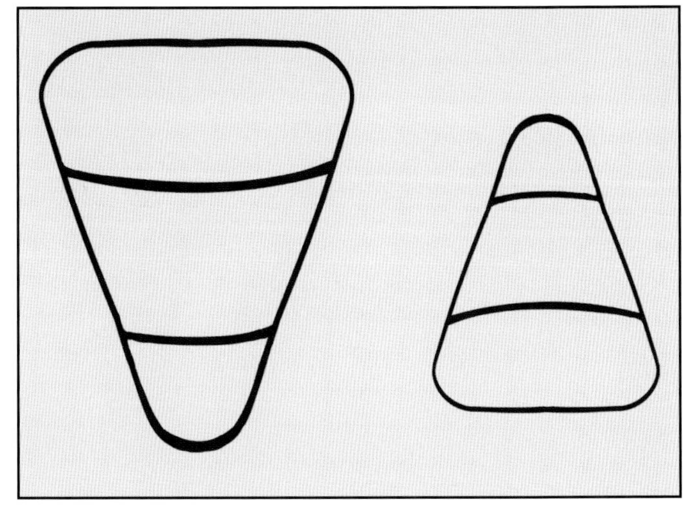

To achieve a finished corn size of 7 in. (as at left) and 5 in. (right), download a template or copy and print this pattern at 600%.

1. Start by tracing your pattern onto the linen, using a lightbox. Be sure to space the candy corn outlines at least 3 in. apart. Using a sewing machine, stitch a close zigzag stitch about ½ in. away from the border of the candy corn. This will keep the backing fabric from fraying after you cut out the hooked portion. I hooked the outline of each color first and then filled in the sections to keep all the tails inside the design.

2. After you have finished hooking, press each candy corn. **(2a)**

   Cut out from the linen. **(2b)**

3. Fold the linen margins back to the reverse of the candy corn pieces and press into place.

2a

2b

1

3

PROJECT 15: CHRISTMAS STOCKING

A Christmas stocking has been on my list to make for many years. This simple, versatile design is classic. I wanted to re-create the look of a feed sack with the stripe and reinforced the idea with a tan feed sack material for the back. The hand-dyed wool in red and green gives the stockings a nice vintage touch. I added the initials for myself and my husband, which is an easy way to customize this pattern.

Lettering has been used in rugs throughout history. While sometimes viewed as difficult, letters are hooked the same as any other loops. A tip I learned from one of my first hooked rugs is to hook the letter into place with a random color that serves as a placeholder. Then fill in the space around the letter, remove the random color, and replace it with your final color. This provides a sharper-looking letter.

Materials & tools needed:

Cotton—½ yd. to line the stocking, or two pieces that are 16 x 20 in.

Feed sack—16 x 20 in. piece

Linen—about 24 x 28 in.

Wool—(amounts are for one stocking, all #9 cut)

- 1/16 td. hand-dyed off-white ("Wooly Sheep")
- ½ yd. hand-dyed off-red ("Redware") or green ("Dark Olive")
- 3–4 strips of dark brown or black for the letter
- 1/32 yd. of hand-dyed tan ("Acorn")

6 in. piece of dark-brown rug binding

Chalk pencil or water/air-soluble fabric pen

Hook + scissors

Needle + thread

Serger (optional)

Sewing machine

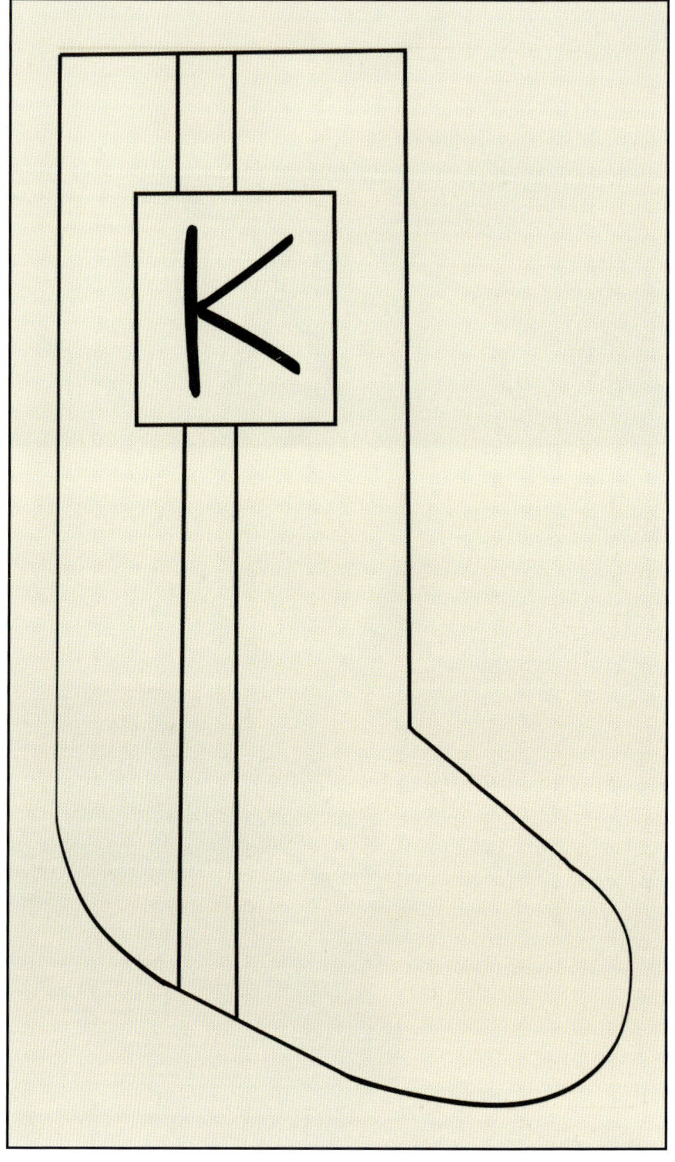

To achieve a finished size of 12 x 18 in., download a template or copy and print this pattern at 300%.

1. Start by drawing the pattern onto your backing fabric, using a lightbox. I hooked my two stockings with intentional vertical rows. This lets the eye travel up and down, giving the stocking a long look. Once you have finished hooking, give the stocking a good press. Then cut it out from the backing fabric, leaving about a 1 in. allowance along all the sides. **(1a)**

   Except the top, which should be 2 in. **(1b)**

2. If you are able to serge the raw edge of your linen, do so.

1a

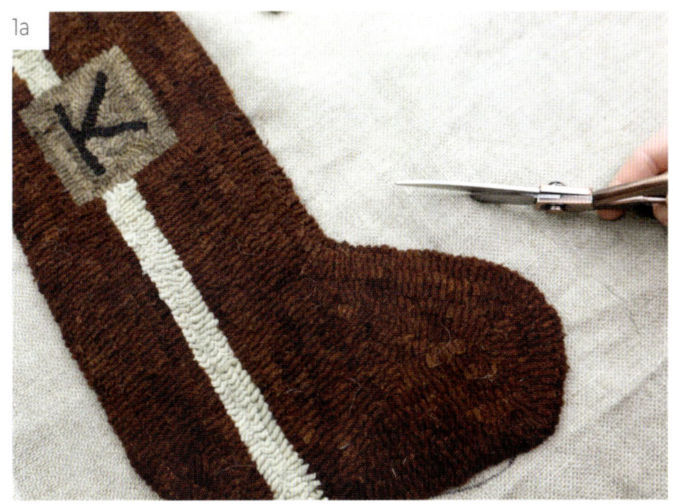

1b

2

3. Lay the stocking right side down on the feed sack (or fabric of choice). I had a striped feed sack fabric, so I lined up the stripe to correspond to the hooked stripe.

4. Pin the sides together on the feed sack side.

5. Using a sewing machine with a zipper foot, stitch as close as you can to the hooked loops.

6. Turn the stocking right side out to ensure that everything is sewn up properly.

7. Turn the stocking inside out and trim any excess seam allowance. If you have a serger, go ahead and serge the seam. Then turn the stocking right side out. Turn the top edge in and press. I did a stay stitch on the feed sack side, since this material did not make a good pressed edge.

8. Take the 6 in. piece of rug binding, fold it in half lengthwise, and stitch it together.

9. Fold the stitched binding in half to form a loop. Stitch this into the heel (left back) side of your stocking, tacking it to the top edge of the stocking and also to the side seam.

10. To make the liner, fold the cotton material right sides together and lay the stocking pattern on top. Trace the stocking outline, using a chalk pencil or water-soluble sewing marker. Make an additional mark ¾ in. from the pattern and 2 in. from the top, for the cutting line. **(10a)**

    Cut out both layers together. Remove the pattern, pin with right sides together, and sew along the traced line. If you have a serger, you can serge the edge of the lining or simply sew another row ¼ in. away from your first row to finish the seam. **(10b)**

3

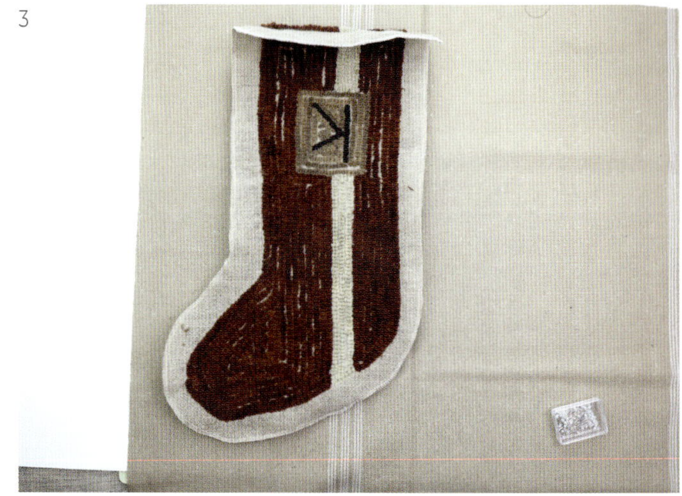

4

5

6
9
7
10a
8
10b

11. Fold over to the outside and press the top edge of the lining about 2 in. down to make a cuff. Then put the lining into the stocking.

12. Pin the top edges of the lining and the stocking together. **(12a)**

    Hand-stitch the lining to the stocking, using a ladder stitch (also known as the slip stitch, blind stitch, or invisible stitch). **(12b)**

    Now make a second stocking—or however many you want—in a complementary color scheme.

11

12a

12b

L
K

Project 16: Tea Cozy

There is nothing better than a large pot of tea on a cold, dreary day. I discovered the wonderful uses of the tea cozy while living in Scotland. It is a traditional British way of keeping a pot of tea warm. This tea cozy will do the perfect job of keeping the pot warm, since wool is a natural insulator.

The most important thing to do is measure your teapot first to ensure the right fit. The design can be worked around the shape. I used both hand sewing and machine sewing to complete this piece. I absolutely love how the project came together with the color of the tea cozy and how it coordinated well with some of my favorite cotton fabric.

To achieve a finished size of 8 x 12 in., download a template or copy and print this pattern at 336%.

Materials & tools needed:

Cotton—30 x 20 in.
Linen—24 x 30 in.
Wool—(cut #8.5)

- Background: 1 yd. hand-dyed light blue ("Melrose")
- Flowers: $^1/_{16}$ yd. white
- Leaves + stems: $^1/_8$ yd. hand-dyed green ("Dark Olive")
- 4 strips of gray
- 3 strips of black
- 3 strips of off-white

Cardstock, the size of one side of your tea cozy
Chalk pencil or water/air-soluble fabric pen
Hook + scissors
Jumbo sewing clips
Needle + strong button thread or upholstery thread
Serger (optional)
Sewing machine
Sharpie

1. Start by measuring your teapot at the highest and the widest points. I used a teapot that was about 7 in. high and about 11 in. wide. I added an inch to each measurement and made my pattern 8 in. high and 12 in. wide. (Check your measurements by cutting out a paper pattern and taping it together to see how it fits over your teapot. It is better to be a little bit too big than too small.)

   Using a lightbox, draw your pattern onto the linen. I started by drawing two 8 x 12 in. rectangles with rounded corners.

   The bee bodies consisted of one tail, one loop, and one tail of black, followed by the same tail, loop, and tail for the yellow, and then one more sequence of black. The wings were the same but hooked at 45° angles to the bee body. Hook your background all around the bee before clipping the tails flush.

Hooking a Beauty Line

2. In this piece I used beauty lines to give the flowers some definition. This is basically adding thin tails between rows of hooking. Find your row of hooking and insert your hooking between the two rows.

3. Pull up a tail.

1

2

3

4. Put your hook back into your fabric right next to your first tail and in the same space between the two rows.

5. Pull up a loop.

6. Cut that loop to form a tail.

7. Cut your tail flush, then smooth them out so they are lying on their sides between the rows.

8. Put your hook in next to the last tail you just made.

9. Pull up a tail.

10. Then pull up another loop, clip that loop, and then cut those two tails flush.

11. Continue this down the row where you wish to add this beauty line.

12. The back of the rug will look like there are little dashes up the row.

13. Once you have finished hooking, give your two pieces a good press. Measure 1 in. around the top and sides, and 2 in. on the bottom. **(13a)**

    Cut the hooked piece out of the backing fabric along the 1 in. and 2 in. marks. **(13b)** (*See overleaf*)

4

5

6

7
10
8
11
9
12

21. Remove the paper, then stitch the cotton with right sides together along the chalk line. Sew only the top and sides, leaving the bottom open. If you are able to serge this seam, do so. Otherwise, you can trim the seam allowance to about $^{3}/_{8}$ in.

22. Fold the bottom of the cotton up about $^{3}/_{4}$ in. and press. Put the cotton into the tea cozy to see how it fits. Adjust the bottom fold if necessary.

23. Pin the bottom of the cotton to the bottom edge of the tea cozy.

24. Using a whip or ladder stitch, attach the cotton to the hooked tea cozy.

22

23

21

24

Project 17: Floral Wine Tote

Everyone will be envious when you attend your next dinner party or picnic with this gorgeous wine tote. As a bonus, this tote is sturdy and will keep the wine chilled. If a wine tote is not your thing, this could easily be made into a pillow, following the instructions for the Wool-Base Flower Pillow project on pages 56–60.

To achieve a finished size of 12 x 13 in., download a template or copy and print this pattern at 366%.

Materials & tools needed:

Linen—24 in. square

Wool—(flowers cut #8, background cut #8.5)

- 1/16 yd. hand-dyed green ("Dark Olive")
- 1/32 yd. hand-dyed yellow ("Colman Mustard Light")
- 1/32 yd. hand-dyed gray/green ("Pebble Green)
- 3 strips of off-white wool
- 3/8 yd. hand-dyed light blue ("Winter Lake")

6 in. circle of fabric—décor or upholstery fabric is the perfect weight for this

13 in. rug binding

1½ x 14 in. leather strap (leather needle for leather might be necessary)

Hook + scissors

Needle + button or upholstery thread

1. Draw a 12 in. (height) x 13 in. (width) rectangle onto your backing fabric. Draw the design in that rectangle. I hooked the flowers and leaves first, followed by the background. When you have finished hooking, press the rug. Then cut it out, leaving 2 in. of linen all the way around. Serge the raw edges.

2. With a sewing machine, attach rug binding to the top edge of the linen.

3. Press the top edge to the back and hand-stitch the edge to the rug.

4. Press the remaining edges to the back of the rug and fold them together so that the two sides match at the corners. Using a ladder stitch (also known as the slip stitch, blind stitch, or invisible stitch), sew up the side from top to bottom.

2

3

1

4

5. For the bottom, take your 6 in. square of décor fabric and press it into a circle with little tucks. Pin this to the bottom of the tote as shown and stitch the two pieces together. This is the hardest part of this piece, so take your time and be patient. For added support on the bottom, I recommend inserting a ¼ in. thick x 4 in. wide, circle of wood.

6. Next add the leather strap. You can adjust this to your preference, but I used a piece of leather that was 14 in. long. **(6a)**

   Because a wine bottle is heavy, you need to secure this strap extremely well. I had about 1½ in. on the inside that I tacked down in all four corners. Take your needle and thread, and stitch from the leather into a seam. **(6b)**

   Work between two rows of hooking and back down so that your threads are not visible on the hooking side. **(6c)**

6a

6b

5

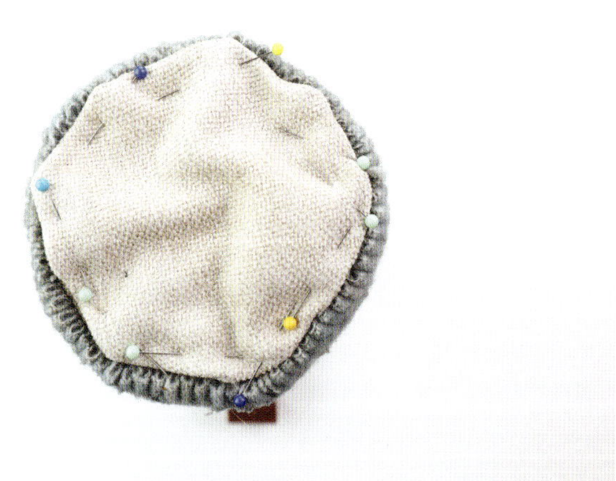

6c

EST.
Domaine
PTERION
2019
RIESLING

4. Take a piece of sandpaper and smooth the edge of the wooden slab so that the hooked rug can curve around the wood and nothing will snag or catch.

5. With the stapler, secure the corners of the rug into place. Make sure the top hooking portion looks even.

6. Work your way around the rug, stapling from one side to the other. (6a)

   Continue stapling until all the linen is securely in place. (6b)

7. Lay the stool on top of your wood, lining up the edges.

8. Using a drill, predrill your holes and secure the stool to the wooden slab. I used five screws: one in the middle and four around the outside.

5

6a

4

6b

7

8

Project 19: Mug Rugs

This project is a very simple and a very quick hook. It is a good project to start out with because the pieces are small. However, I have added it to the end of the book because it is also a great way to use up your extra scraps and "worms." The amount of wool needed for each is minimal, and it's a great way to stretch your creativity without being too demanding. The mug rugs make lovely coasters for a hot tea or cocoa and could be a great housewarming gift. These mug rugs would also pair well with the tea cozy project.

Materials & tools needed:

- Linen—15 in. square easily makes four rugs
- Wool—any leftover scraps or worms. If you are brave, you could choose randomly for an unexpected result.
- Hook + scissors
- Sewing needle + thread
- Thick fabric for backing—scraps of upholstery fabric make excellent backs for these coasters.

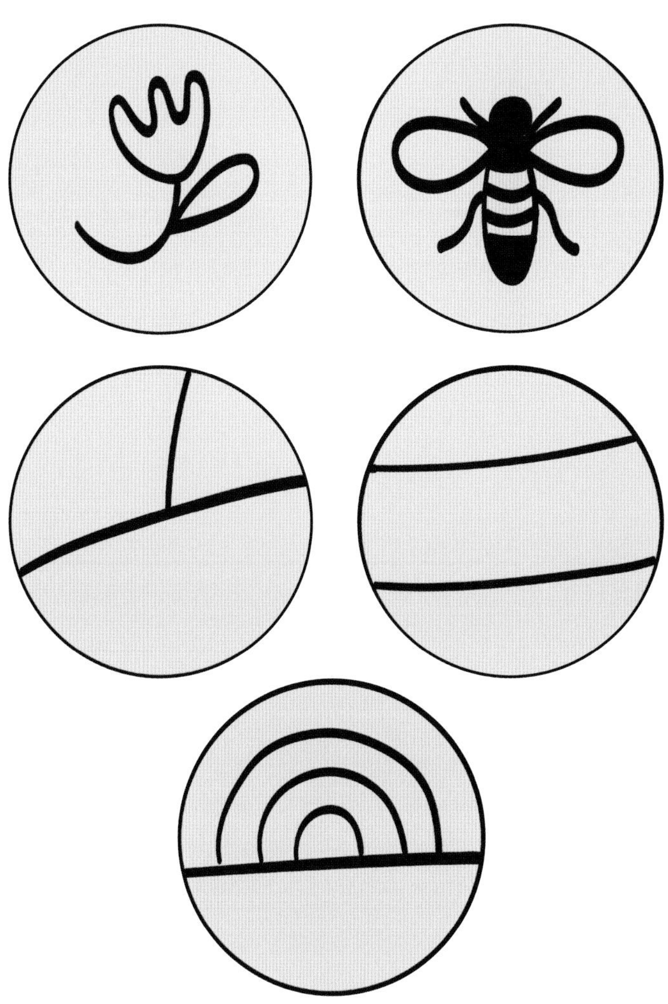

To achieve a finished individual diameter of 4 in., download a template or copy and print each pattern at 247%.

1. Draw circles onto your backing fabric. I used a 4 in. wood cutout that I had on hand. Otherwise, the bottom of a jar, another round coaster, or even an embroidery hoop would do the trick as well. I zigzagged ½ in. from the drawn circle before I started hooking, to keep the backing fabric from fraying. They can be serged after you have finished hooking as well.

2. Press your piece as you would any other rug. Then, trim away the excess backing fabric—leave about 2 in. around the edge. You will need to hook all the coasters before you start to cut out any of them. I hooked this mug rug in straight lines. I did not want the tails to be at the edge of the hooked mat, so I left them on the back. This works because the back of the mat will be covered with a piece of fabric.

3. Press the excess backing fabric to the back of your coaster.

1

2

3

4. Draw the same circles on your backing fabric four times.

5. Cut the circles out for each coaster.

6. Pin the cutout circles to each of your coasters.

7. Using whip stitch, sew the coasters to the fabric circles. **(7a)**

   Whip-stitch the other three coasters as well. **(7b)**

   Give the pieces one final press on completion. **(7c)**

6

4

7a

5

7b

7c

About the Author

Katie Kriner took her first rug-hooking class over ten years ago. She started hooking designs by other artists but soon found that most designs did not fit her style. Through various classes and camps, she developed her skills, designed patterns, color-planned, and dyed wool for her own rugs. From there she found a niche in helping customers and friends do the same for their own rugs. Katie currently owns a shop called The Bee & The Bear, where she focuses on teaching and selling rug-hooking supplies. Most of the pieces she designs and makes are either for her home and personal use or for friends and family. She is a lifelong gardener, which serves as inspiration for much of her work. Katie lives in southeastern Pennsylvania with her husband and German shepherd. Visit her website at www.thebeethebear.com.

Acknowledgments

A big thank-you to Jo Bryant and BlueRed Press for believing that I had something to share. Thanks to the many people at Schiffer Publishing for your invaluable input and helping me publish this book.

A book like this would never have come about without all of the love and support from my family, friends, and customers, many of whom have become friends as well. Thanks to the Thursday gals who have cheered me on from the first day I opened the doors to my little shop. I would not be here without you. Thanks to Denise Chantelau for helping me hook and finish several projects as I neared the end. Thanks to my mom and Cherilyn Howard for thoroughly reading through the many pages of instructions and helping me best explain the steps for each project.

I am especially thankful for the teaching and friendship of Kay Leisey, who started me on my rug-hooking journey. A big thank-you to Megan Detwiler of Megan Ashley Photography for all the photography help. To my parents, thank you for always encouraging me and being my biggest cheerleaders. Your love and support have been invaluable to every aspect of my life, especially this rug-hooking journey. And to my husband, Lucas, thank you for all of the love and support throughout this business journey and life. From the many hours we spent editing the prose to the discussions on the designs and colors, this book is better for your input and help.

References & Resources

General Rug History and Other Information

Kopp, Joel and Kate. *American Hooked and Sewn Rugs, Folk Art Underfoot*. Dutton Adult, 1985.

Turbayne, Jessie A. *Hooked Rugs: History and the Continuing Tradition*. Schiffer Publishing, 1997.

Techniques & Inspiration

Boswell, Thom. *The Rug Hook Book: Techniques, Projects and Patterns for This Easy Traditional Craft*. Sterling, 1992.

Darr, Tara. *Wool Rug Hooking: Pillows, Footstools, Rugs*. Krause Publications, 2005.

Finishing Hooked Rugs: Favorite Techniques from the Experts. Rug Hooking Magazine, 2013.

Hooked Carpetbags, Handbags & Totes. Rug Hooking Magazine, 2017.

Jamar, Tracy. *Coils, Folds, Twists, and Turns: Contemporary Techniques in Fiber*. Stackpole Books, 2017.

Lovelady, Donna. *Rug Hooking for the First Time*. Sterling/Chapelle, 2003.

Miller, Kris. *Introduction to Rug Hooking: A Beginners Guide to Tools, Techniques & Materials*. Rug Hooking Magazine, 2015.

Olson, Jane and Shepherd, Gene. *The Rug Hooker's Bible*. Rug Hooking Magazine, 2006.